A RashDash and Northern Stage co-production
in association with Soho Theatre

TWO MAN SHOW

A RashDash production, co-commissioned by Northern Stage and Soho Theatre and supported by Arts Council England and the Golsoncott Foundation.

Created and performed by RashDash and Becky Wilkie
Written by Abbi Greenland and Helen Goalen
Music by Becky Wilkie
Lyrics by RashDash and Becky Wilkie

Two Man Show was originally performed at Northern Stage, Summerhall 6th August 2016 with the following company:

Abbi / John	Abbi Greenland
Helen / Dan	Helen Goalen
Goddess / Musician	Becky Wilkie
Designer	Oliver Townsend
Lighting Designer	Katharine Williams
Stage Manager	Simon Perkins
Producer	Charlotte Bennett
Exhibition Designers	Elisa Nader and Rosie Gibbons

Thanks for talking to us/working with us/bearing with us
Jo Clifford, James Blakey, Victor Lambert, Matt Randall, Penny Greenland, Ian Heywood, Heather Long, Luke Thompson, Lorne Campbell, Gary Kitching, Matt Howden, Di Barnes, Laurence Cook, Chris Thorpe, Jo Somner, Elisa Nader, Rosie Gibbons, Fred Thomas, Emma Wilkie.

Thanks for donating to our Crowdfund
Alex, David Somner, Alison Ford, Marie Keyworth, Frances Haigh, Victor Lambert, Malcolm Raeburn, Isabella Marshall, Bettrys Jones, Karis McDonald, Jon Brittain, Katie Turner, Chloe Green, Terrence Rae, Jonathan Miles, Meghan Doyle, Andrew Hughes, Olivia Lamont, Ben Schofield, Harry Hepple, Ben Clare, Susan Wokoma, Rod Thomas, Rich Rusk, Katie Lyons, James Phillips, Elaine Goodfellow, Zosh Skowronska, Lauren King, Sara, Jimi Mitchell, Alan Lane, Lucy Hind, Adam Charteris, Laurence Cook, Beatrice Ray, Florence Hall, Richard Smith, Jo Herbert, Lizzie Franks, Allan Wilson, Sean Casey, Helena Lymbery, Ian Heywood and a lot of anonymous supporters.

TWO MAN SHOW

RashDash

TWO MAN SHOW

OBERON BOOKS
LONDON

WWW.OBERONBOOKS.COM

First published in 2017 by Oberon Books Ltd
521 Caledonian Road, London N7 9RH
Tel: +44 (0) 20 7607 3637 / Fax: +44 (0) 20 7607 3629
e-mail: info@oberonbooks.com
www.oberonbooks.com

PB ISBN: 9781786821317
E ISBN: 9781786821324

Cover image by The Other Richard

The show is performed by two actors/dancers
and one musician.

Character names are indicated by initials in the script.

Abbi and Helen are the names of the original makers/
performers and could be substituted for the names of
performers of future shows.

/ Indicates an overlapping of text.

The use of a full stop on a line on its own suggests a pause.

Words in [ ] are not spoken.

Notes on the movement scenes/sketches

To express a movement in all its character and truth, it is important that it be at once the result of the successive moments that have preceded the moment that one has fixed, and that it announces the sensations of those that follow. (Rodin)

The sketches in this text represent the movement scenes. We have decided that sketches of a few moments rather than photographs or choreographic notation get us closest to the essence of what these scenes are and what they do. The sketches are not here to act as a blueprint for future productions or accurately capture the first production, but to give a glimpse of what we feel is important about those scenes. It is important that the movement scenes are given as much time and space in the production as the text.

Notes from Oliver Townsend
the artist/designer of the show

This was a really enjoyable exercise in drawing. Sketching with an intention to align something in the feeling of the drawings to the experience of watching you both...glimpses of anatomy amidst motion and the feeling that you're watching something that is delicate and articulate and muscular and ferocious and primal and hilarious and poignant and so much more... forgetting the gender thing and then remembering it, forgetting the nakedness and then remembering it, forgetting there's a story and then remembering it...and primarily not wanting to over-simplify the spirit of the show by making objective decisions with lines on paper! And not wanting to draw in a classical anatomical way by accident! And wanting to allow lines in your poses to become slightly like the earth goddesses we looked at! And not wanting to give too much away! And And And...

The earth goddess we looked at…

Miriam is aware of the atmosphere of the table rather than of the table – she doesn't describe what it looks like but how it feels.
From Virginia Wolf's essay, Dorothy Richardson and the woman's sentence

Whose voice is speaking those words? Whose voice has always spoken? Deafening tumult of important voices; and not one a woman's voice. I haven't forgotten the names of the great talkers. Plato, Aristotle and Montaigne, Marx and Freud and Nietzsche. I know them because I've lived among them and among them alone. These strong voices are also those who have reduced me the most effectively to silence. It is these superb speakers who, more than any others, have forced me into silence.

How can it be that we are now coming out of our coma, and that our tongues, still sticky with respect for your values, are loosening up, slowly?
Annie Leclerc (translated by Clare Duchen) Woman's Word

I am a God
Kanye West, *I am a God*

PROLOGUE

A: For two million nine hundred and ninety thousand years men and women were equal.

H: Warning: What we are about to say may completely contradict everything you think you know, even though you may not really know why you think you know it. But don't worry you can trust us. Because we know everything.

A: Warning: We're going to go quite fast now. Don't worry if it's all a bit much, you can always google it after the show.

H: For two million nine hundred and ninety thousand years men and women were equal.

A: They lived in hunter gatherer societies and they moved from place to place, hunting and gathering.

H: One day, someone noticed the link between seed and grain. Seed that fell on the ground near the cooking pot, became grain the following season.

Agriculture begins. Humans begin to settle.

A: This was the neolithic time and it was peaceful!

During this time There Were Goddesses.

During this time women were the high priestesses although we weren't called that then.

During this time it was women who were buried in the best spots.

We know this because of archaeology.

H: Then. It happened. The Goddesses were crushed by Sky Gods and men took over religion.

A: People have suggested many reasons for this. But before the beginning there was the truth and the truth was this:

There was a time when we weren't conscious that
One day we will All Die.

There was a time when we didn't have the concepts of
Dominance or Power.

There was a time when we didn't know that Sex or Men
had anything to do with Making the Babies. We knew
that sometimes they would come out of a vagina, but
we did not know how they'd gotten up there in the first
place.

This changed.

H: First: In the palaeolithic times we learn that we die.
It is frightening. We invent the afterlife, to make it
less frightening.

A: Second: In the neolithic times, children become
important because we need more labour for our
agriculture. Making Babies therefore becomes very
important, and with that, the Women who Make them.

H: Third: After we have invented plant farming, we invent
animal farming. The relationship between the farmer and
the animal is the first ever to contain dominance. The
animal that had been the hunter's equal in a battle of wit
and speed becomes the farmer's slave. We learn that we
can control other living things if we want to. To do this we
learn to think of them as less. We learn power.

A: Fourth: After we have domesticated the animals, we
want to breed the animals and for this we need to
understand where the babies come from. We watch.
We learn. We see for the first time that Men and Sex
are in fact necessary for making babies. Sex is no
longer just for funsies. Men are no longer surplus to our
reproductive requirements.

H: Fifth: We decide that in animal farming the male animal
is less valuable than the female. Only one strong male

is required for copulation, the rest are killed for meat or castrated and used to draw the plough.

Animal castration during this time is very painful. We will now give graphic details.

GODDESS: Practices included opening the scrotum with a knife to remove the testicles or damaging or destroying the testicles while they were still attached. Damaging or destroying practices included tying the testicles off with string so they atrophied slowly, crushing the testicles between two elongated stones, or wrapping the testicles in cloth and then biting or chewing them off. This results in infertile males that are more docile and easy to handle.

H: All this frightened the men. Obviously.

These developments are important because of how they combine in the male human.

A: ONE: The male human is frightened of death. The male human learns he is essential to reproduction. The male human decides that he can beat death by siring offspring. The male human needs to know which offspring sprung from him, and which offspring sprung from other male humans. The male human conceives of chastity and fidelity; the cornerstones of the patriarchy.

H: TWO: The male human conceives of dominance. The male human learns that his penis is essential to making babies. The male human's essential penis comes under threat from other bigger, stronger men with more essential penises. The male human fears he will die an insignificant and irrelevant blip. The male human doesn't have to take this lying down.

H: I can hear you thinking 'alright then little girl, if you like your prehistory so much maybe we should take away your fancy lights and your electric guitar'.

A: I can hear you thinking 'but what about the monkeys? Don't they organise themselves into natural patriarchies? Didn't David Attenborough or some other

17

softly spoken voice of male authority tell me this? How could you challenge David? He's got a boat named after him and everything.' Well actually, no they don't.

H: Chimpanzees don't, baboons don't, macaques don't, gibbons, gorillas, rhesus monkeys, all don't.

A: After thousands of years of watching monkeys from within the safety of our patriarchal hierarchies it won't surprise you to discover that we've misread and misused evidence to set examples for our bad behaviour.

H: Their behaviour is far more nuanced and far less fucked up that we give them credit for.

A: We could go into this because as you know we know everything but it would be long and pretty soon we intend to stop declaiming and start telling you a story about the crisis of masculinity because as you know we know everything and are fully qualified and have the ideal life experience to dissect and discuss this issue.

H: People have said that patriarchy is natural.

A: People have said that patriarchy is the natural result of the male animal's superior strength.

H: People have said that the female is universally submissive to the male.

When the male animal 'mounts' the female, neither he nor she can possibly conceive of dominance or possession. These are human inventions.

The male human's secondary though essential role in reproduction makes his existence feel precarious and vulnerable.

A: This is a song about patriarchy

It springs from fear
It springs from fear
It springs from fear, do you hear?
Do you hear? Do you hear?

It is not natural
Not inevitable
Not desirable desirable desirable

So
Move over
It's done

This
Is taking
Too long

So
Move over
It's done

This
Is taking
Too long

There was a time
When there were goddesses
So peaceful
There was a time, there was a time

It springs from fear
It is not natural
Do you hear? Do you hear?
Not desire desire desire desire desirable

So
Move over
It's done

This
Is taking
Too long

So
Move over
It's done

This
Is taking
Too long

A & H: Male humans. You have nothing to fear.
You are wonderful. We love you. We respect you.
You are visionaries, but you are also destroyers and
I can see that you are struggling, like we are.

Music and movement.

SCENE ONE

John enters. Dan is already there.

J: Shit

D: Sorry

J: You made me jump

D: I thought about calling ahead but then I just. Didn't and –

J: Well it's your home too, so –

D: Well. Not really, but –

J: Nah, but you know what I mean

D: Yeah, yeah I know

J: You're welcome anytime

D: Thanks

J: It doesn't have to be Christmas or anything

D: No

J: Not that you come at Christmas, but –

D: Well no I didn't last year 'cause I was –

J: No I know, at thingy's parents –

D: Sarah's

J: Sarah's parents yeah I remember we don't have to –

D: Right yeah.

J: It's nice to see you

D: Yeah, you too, it's good.

.

J: I didn't see your car

D: Didn't you?

J: No I didn't see it

D: I parked it on the street

J: I would've walked past it though

D: I've got a Lexus now

J: That black one?

D: Yeah I didn't want to get it covered in shit, so I just, / parked and walked

J: / That's a nice car

D: Yeah it's not bad

J: Must've cost you a fair bit

D: My mate got me a good deal

J: Nice

.

D: I thought you'd be in when I got here because of...

J: I went out to get milk

D: Oh. Is it alright to leave him?

J: It was only fifteen minutes. Did you go in and see him?

D: No. I didn't know if that would be a good idea so I just.

.

J: How's it going?

D: Yeah good

J: How's Sarah?

D: She's good, yeah

J: And work?

D: Going pretty smooth

J: That's all good, then.

D: ~~Yeah. Yourself?~~

J: ~~Fine yeah~~

D: Anything new?

J: ~~Not really~~

D: Still playing footy?

J: When someone can be in for Dad on a Sunday morning, yeah

D: Course, scored much?

J: I've saved some, because, I play in goal but, no scoring, no

D: Right yeah. You're looking pretty trim

J: Thanks

D: You must be working out a bit

J: I keep busy

D: Me too actually yeah. I met this guy at my gym that's like, he's not that big, but he's fucking strong. Went pretty far in Ninja Warrior last year. He's been sorting me out

J: Sounds decent

D: Says that it's all about core strength, not all of this protein powder bench-pressing shit you know

J: Right

D: What've you got there?

J: Protein shake

D: Right. Well, you're a big guy I guess so, makes sense for you. Beefing up and that.

J: Each to their own.

.

D: How is he?

J: It's fine for you to see him, he might be sleeping, / but

D: / Yeah, but, just before I go in. Is he...you know...
alright?

J: Yeah

D: Has he got any worse?

J: Since when?

D: Last time

J: Last time was like, over a year ago... so, yeah it'll be
a bit different. But. It's probably easier if you just see.

D: Cool. Is it bad?

J: Well he's not dead yet and it's gonna get worse, so –

D: I'll go and see him in a minute

J: Whenever you're ready

D: Oh I'm ready, I'm fine, it's just, I don't want to, you
know...agitate him.

J: Agitate?

D: Yeah

J: Cool

.

J: Your phone's ringing again

D: Yeah. How's Hannah?

J: She's alright

D: Where is she?

J: Don't know. You do know this is like the fifth time though, right?

D: You broke up?

J: Yeah

D: When?

J: Couple of months ago now

D: Ah that's a shame what happened?

J: She got bored I think

D: Of what?

J: Hanging out with me and my incontinent dad

D: Incontinent?

J: Yeah

D: That's new

J: Is it?

D: That wasn't happening last time

J: Right

D: When did that start?

J: Not sure exactly

D: You don't know?

J: I don't keep a diary, no

D: What do the doctors say?

J: Not much

D: Can't they do anything?

J: Like what?

D: Make it go into a bag or something?

J: No

D: Why are you so calm about it?

J: Why are you so bothered it's not you that has to deal with it

D: Who does?

J:

D: What about the nurse?

J: She comes, like, once a week

D: So you...you know?

J: Yeah.

.

J: Whoever it is, is pretty keen to speak to you, Dan

D: I'll call her back later

J: Everything alright?

D: Yeah, she's just being a bit, clingy

J: Right

D: Can you answer it and say I'm with Dad or something?

J: I've never met her so that might be a bit weird

D: Haven't you?

J: No

D: You should come and meet her sometime

J: Or you could bring her here

D: No way

J: Why not?

D: I dunno, just, no.

J: You ashamed of your Hulk duvet cover?

D: ~~Is that still up there?~~

J: Ready and waiting

D: This place is turning into a shithole. You need to get some new stuff

J: Yeah well you're turning into a shithole and you need to get some new. Stuff.

Yeah I fucked it

D: It's alright mate, speed's never been your strong point

J: Shall we go outside and have a race then, Dan?

D: That's not what I meant.

J: Oh sorry, it's just so hard to keep up with your mental agility these days

.

D: Look, can you answer it and if it's not an emergency just tell her I'll call her back later

J: What counts as an emergency?

D: I dunno, everything. Since she got pregnant it's like an emergency if she's hungry

J: She's pregnant?

D: Yeah

J: Well that's a pretty big deal, Dan

D: I guess

J: Congratulations

D: Thanks

J: Is it yours?

D: Course it's mine

J: Well you didn't say anything I didn't know if it was –
sorry. What is it?

D: Boy

J: Cool

D: Yeah

J: When's it due?

D: Four months

J: That's pretty soon

D: Yep

J: I'm gonna be an uncle

Deano just had a baby

D: Deano's a nutter

J: I think it might be good for him. Rabs had one last year
and it's really chilled him out. He's always telling us
funny stuff it says. Could be a laugh

D: It's just gonna be changing nappies and staying in

J: Yeah that would be shit wouldn't it.

.

D: I think she's given up

.

J: I'm gonna check on Dad, do you want to come?

D: Yeah yeah, I'll just sort this, and I'll be in in a minute

J: He'll be happy to see you

D: No he won't

J: Yes he will

J: He's not going to remember who you are.

SCENE TWO

The performers take off their clothes, they wear pants and nothing else.

Music and movement.

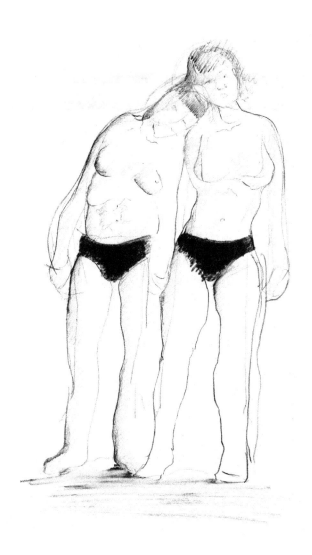

Also
notes of
evidence

SCENE THREE

D: When I am a billionaire, I shall erect a fifty foot statue to commemorate. Blank.

J: Blank

D: Yeah, you fill in the blank

J: Gandhi

D: Right

J: Is that right?

D: Well, it's not wrong, but it's not really about getting it right, it's –

J: So what's the point?

D: Well it's supposed to be funny

J: When is Gandhi ever funny?

D: Well, he would be funny, if, for example, I'd asked the question 'How did I lose my virginity?' 'Gandhi' or 'What did Vin Diesel eat for dinner?' See. On the black cards. The question cards.

J: Right. So I can't just say anything?

D: Anything funny or offensive from the white cards, which I've given you. / That's what you can say.

J: / But what if I can think of something that's more offensive than any of the cards?

D: No. It's got to be ironic or you're just being a cunt. So. I ask a question from the black card, which is, When I am a billionaire, I shall erect a fifty foot statue to commemorate –

J: What's queefing?

D: Fanny farts

J: How would I make a statue of that?

D: ~~Well you can choose any card, there might be~~ better cards, but with that one, the fact that it's not immediately obvious how you would turn it into a statue might be part of why it's funny. So, how would you make a statue of a queef?

J: That's funny to you?

D: Well not right now, because we're analysing it, but when you're playing properly that could be funny yes

J: How are we not playing properly?

D: You're supposed to have more than two players, and you win the round by saying the funniest or most offensive thing / so it gets a bit more –

J: / Alright. Child Abuse.

D: Child Abuse. Right. Is that on a card?

J: Yes

D: So you're saying that, when you're a billionaire, you're going to erect a fifty foot statue to commemorate Child Abuse

J: Yes. Do I win?

D: We're not really playing to win / but yeah, I guess so

J: / I mean it would be hard to commemorate something that still happens, / but

D: / Yeah

J: So maybe I should choose a different one

D: Er. / Alright but

J: / Like Daniel Radcliffe's Delicious Asshole. Is that better?

D: Yep

J: Some of these are a bit sick, Dan

D: We don't have to play

J: No it's alright, you clearly like it so I'm sure I can get into it.

.

D: What do you think would happen if we went out and left him? Just for an hour or two?

J: Don't know

D: He might sleep the whole time

J: He might

D: What's the worst that could happen?

J: He could wake up, not know where he is, try to get up to go for a piss, fall over and break something, have a heart attack or a stroke and then die slowly in a pool of his own sick and shit.

D: Right. Are we playing or not?

J: I'm choosing

D: You're taking your time

J: Sorry did you need to rush off again Dan?

.

D: Have you smoked already today?

J: Yeah

D: It's pretty early

J: Did you want some?

D: Is it alright to be high when you're, you know, here and –

J: That's right you don't want to whitey again

D: Every single time. I was fourteen

~~**J:** It was fucking funny~~

~~**D:** Good~~

J: Funnier than child abuse anyway

~~**D:** We don't have to play~~

J: No I've got one, I'm ready. I get by with a little help from. Blank.

.

D:

J: What?

D: Nothing

.

D: I get by with a little help from. Blank.

J: Yeah

D: Okay.

J: You started thinking of names yet?

D: No

J: What about John?

D: Good idea

J: Easy to remember. Your dad, your brother and your son all called John. Simple.

D: John isn't your real name

J: Everyone calls me John but you

D: Your name is Terrence

J: That doesn't piss me off

D: I'm not trying to piss you off

J: John pisses you off

D: It's a nickname

J: I could change it officially if you wanted me to

D: So you could be even more like him?

J: I'm not like him

D: Yes you are, Little John

J: I'm bigger than you

D: I know what you're doing

J: What am I doing?

D: Trying to draw me in

J: Is that what your counsellor says?

D: I don't see a counsellor

J: Anymore

D: You saw her too

J: Once. I didn't go back because talking doesn't fucking / solve anything

D: / Getting Really High

J: I had three puffs / like an hour ago

D: / No. That's my answer. I get by with a little help from Getting Really High.

J: Choose a better one

D: Repression

J: That's not on a fucking card

D: Yeah it is, look

J: Fuck

D: Alright my turn. Daddy, why is Mommy crying?

J: Fine

D: So now you choose the funniest answer

J: Or the most offensive, right?

D: Right. Daddy, Why is Mommy crying?

J: Yeah I heard you, it's just hard to choose between these two

D: What are they?

J: Your Weird Brother or A Defective Condom

D: That's the best you've got?

J: I've got ten cards, what've you got, Dan?

D: A Lifetime Of Sadness

J: How about An Oedipus Complex

D: Do you even know what that is?

J: Are you fucking kidding me?

D: Just because I liked Mum better than Dad

J: She didn't have long enough to do anything wrong,
/ of course you liked her better

D: / You barely remember her, don't pretend like you know

J: You weren't easy, Dan

D: I played the clarinet and read comics in my room all day.

J: Fucking exactly

D: What's he been saying to you?

J: He hasn't spoken in full sentences for a year so not much

D: Then why are you defending him?

J: What's your problem, you think you can do any better?

D: No I don't. Can we play the game?

.

J: What is there a ton of in heaven?

D: Dead Fathers.

.

D: What is Batman's guilty pleasure?

.

J: Hospice Care

.

J: Instead of coal, Santa gives the bad children. Blank.

D: The Miracle of Childbirth?

.

J: Shall we stop?

D: Yeah

J: Do you want to get a takeaway?

D: It's 11.30

J: Yeah but I'm hungry for chow mein

D: Isn't that breaking your diet?

J: Fuck off, Dan

D: Yeah alright

SCENE FOUR

The performers sing a classical vocal medley featuring some of the world's greatest male composers of the last four hundred years. During this they become fully naked.

Music and movement.

SCENE FIVE

J: Where've you been?

D: The attic

J: All morning?

D: I went for a run earlier

J: I tried to / call you

D: / Do you remember DJ Shadow? Fuck I miss being able to play your music really loud without anyone posting passive aggressive notes through your door. Look what I found

J: You set the school record for discus throwing in year nine

D: I did

J: That's really good

D: Dad wouldn't put it on the wall because the previous record had been set by a girl

J: That wasn't why

D: Yeah it was

J: It was the same week you were grounded for bringing that magazine home

D: That was your magazine

J: I did tell him that

D: Did you?

J: He said you should take the responsibility because you're older

D: No what he actually said was it should have been my magazine. Apparently the magazine was fine, what wasn't fine was that you got hold of it first.

J: I don't remember that bit

D: You got it from Fudge

J: What's Fudge?

D: Tall, skinny guy that used to hang around outside the shop

J: You mean Kevin who sets fire to stuff?

D: We called him Fudge because he said that's what his GCSE results spelled

J: I didn't think you could get a G?

D: Yeah but he was dyslexic and no one told him he'd got it wrong

J: You know, he died last year

D: What?

J: Jumped off the bridge

D: Why?

J: No one knows. But he must've been pretty sure 'cause he aimed for the fucking road

D: Shit

J: Good funeral though

D: Can a funeral be good?

J: Do you want to sit down?

D: No I'm alright just now

J: I think you should sit down.

D: What's happened?

J: Dad died this morning.

.

D: What?

.

D: Why didn't you tell me?

J: You were happy about your discus thing

D: So?

J: Yeah maybe that was weird. I don't know.

D: What happened?

J: His heart stopped

D: When?

J: This morning

D: He was here last night

J: Yeah

D: You don't seem surprised

J: I am. I just. I don't know.

D: What happened?

J: I went in to give him some breakfast and he wasn't breathing, so, I called an ambulance

D: Was he dead already?

J:

D: Why didn't you call me?

J: I did

D: Shit

J: I don't think it's that bad that you weren't there though

D: Yes it fucking is

J: No, because you don't like him

D: I do like him. I do, I did, I don't know but I should have. I would have been there when he. Where is he?

J: At the hospital. Do you want to go and see him?

D: No.

Are you alright?

J: Yeah. Are you?

D: I don't know

J: Do you want to. Talk about it?

D: I think we probably should

J: Right

D: I think we should hug first though, what do you think?

J: Yeah whatever you want.

They hug.

J: I don't really know what you want me to say now

D: We could say nice memories?

J: Alright, you got any?

D: I don't know. Have you?

J: Yeah probably

.

D: You liked him teaching you how to drive... didn't you? You said he was funny

.

D: Or, uh... Maccy D's after football? What would he always get? A Happy Meal?

J: No, just a Big Mac

D: Oh I thought there was something funny once with a toy?

J: That was Uncle Dave

D: Oh yeah. Uncle Dave.

     .

D: Do you think he knows. Knew. What was going on?
     Was he thinking things?

J: When you make eye contact with him he does that little –.
     Yeah he knows.

D: Knew

J: Yeah

D: Any stories?

J: Not really, just funny stuff 'cause he's demented

D: Was

J: Whatever

D: Say one

J: No

D: Go on, say one you could say at his funeral

J: He doesn't want us to say anything at his funeral

D: What?

J: He planned it and paid for it ages ago. He doesn't want
     anyone to say anything, he's being cremated and we
     can do what we like with his ashes.

     What?

D: He doesn't want anyone to say anything because he
     doesn't trust us to say what he wants. I'm surprised he
     didn't write the fucking speech himself. And if he was
     that organised he could have done something useful
     and gifted us his money and his house six months ago
     so we didn't have to pay shit loads of tax.

J: Fuck, Dan

.

D: ~~What?~~

J: You're a cunt

D: ~~You're a cunt~~

J: No, you are such a fucking cunt /

D: / Fuck you

J: He brought you up. He did his best. He made you who you are

D: Exactly

J: He was right, you're a little pussy boy.

Look at your fucking life and your wife and your – Piss off back home and have your perfect little kid.

D: I don't want a kid

J: Well it's a bit late for that now

D: No it's not

J: So what, you're just gonna leave them?

D: It'd be better for the kid

J: Pussy boy

D: She shouldn't have it.

.

J: Have you said that to her?

D:

J: What did she say?

D: She wants it

J: Well then.

D: Well what?

J: You know what.

D: Why isn't it my choice too?

J: Why are you such a cunt?

D: If I was a cunt then I would have a say in my own
fucking life.

.

He taught me how to throw okay. I'm not awful at
throwing and he taught me how to throw.

J: You are awful at throwing

D: Fuck off John. Who gives a shit about throwing anyway?

J: Yeah that's right

D: Is there still loads of whisky in the shed?

J: Yeah

D: You got ice?

J: No

D: Whatever.

SCENE SIX

Music. JOHN and DAN drink, dance and fight.

scene 6 : super primal

SCENE SEVEN

D: ~~Fuckfuckfuckfuckfuckfuckfuck~~

J: What?

D: John I've really fucked this

J: ~~What?~~

D: I can't tell you

J: Alright then

D: What's wrong with you?

J: What?

D: You're just going to leave it there?

J: You said you don't want to talk about it?

D: I know but you're supposed to make me!

J: What? Now?

D: Yes now

J: Alright. What's happened?

D: I can't tell you

J: Well that's fine

D: John!

J: Do you want to write it down?

D: No. Because then it'll be real

J: What is it?

D: I didn't call Sarah

J: I know

D: No. I didn't call Sarah back and she. She thought. She thought.

J: What?

D: I

.

.

J: You told her you didn't want it and she's –

D: Oh god

I didn't know what I was saying. She knows I say stuff I don't mean. She should have fucking known! She should have known.

J: Dan, is she alright?

D: She won't stop crying. Her mum keeps calling me and leaving me voicemails. Sarah told her it was her choice. But I know she knows.

There's a reason it should be her fucking choice. Everyone knows that. What's wrong with her?

.

That was my son.

J: Don't, Dan.

D: What has she done to my son?

J: Shut up Dan.

D: Or what? You gonna punch me?

J: Stop it.

D: You gonna put all that chicken and broccoli and punchbags and fucking protein shakes to good use finally?

J: You think that if I punch you you'll feel better? Well you won't and you don't deserve to

D: Since when did you do pop psychology?

J: I'm not an idiot

D: ~~You're so hung up on thinking I think you're an idiot~~

J: ~~No, I don't give a shit what you think of me~~

D: You're not clever though are you?

J: ~~Go take a cold shower, Dan.~~

D: Oh it's the new caring John now. Little John doesn't punch anymore. Little John changes nappies and cuddles his daddy / and cooks Nigella recipes. Little John has become Little Jane.

J: / I know what you're trying to do and I don't give a shit

D: Are you so removed from any kind of social life that you can't even punch anymore?

J: No. I'm a man, not a little boy

D: You're a cliché, John, listen to yourself. And I'd rather be a little boy because little boys can fucking cry. Now punch me so at least my eyes water

J: Punch yourself.

D: If she was the strong empowered woman she says she is she should have decided to have it on her own. She shouldn't need me to help her bring up a kid if she's such a / fucking feminist!

J: / Maybe it's not about doing it alone. Maybe she did it for you. Maybe she's already got one fucking kid and she can't have another

D: How do you know any of this?

J: I don't

D: Have you been talking to her?

J: Dan, we've never met

D: I imagine you fucking her sometimes. I'll be at work and I'll imagine you fucking her and I'm in the / wardrobe watching and I don't say anything

J: / Stop telling me things that make you sound so pathetic I cannot bear it

D: What are you gonna do now, John? Now you don't have to look after the monster? You'll have to get a job. You can't pretend you're being useful anymore. You'll have no excuse not to see anyone. You'll have no excuse for staying locked in this stupid, shitty house. You probably can't even afford to stay with all they're going to tax you and I could help you, but you wouldn't ask me. So I won't.

J: I've got a funeral to go to. I take it you're not coming?

D: No. And it's a real shame. I won't be able to do the speech I'd prepared about my amazing father and inspiration.

J: You were never going to come

D: How do you know?

J: You packed your car before Sarah rang you. I saw you this morning. You were gonna go back weren't you?

D: No

J: Yeah you were. You were going to go back and make it right weren't you?

D:

J: You took just too long to decide you're a decent person now fucking look.

D: Maybe if he'd died a day earlier, everything would be alright.

.

J: I'm gonna call a taxi

D: You should wear a suit more often

J: I can't move

D: You look like a man.

.

J: Will you be here when I get back?

D: Don't know

J: Good luck

John exits.

D: You used to be funny

You're not funny anymore.

Music.

SCENE EIGHT

Helen goes to start the next dance scene. Abbi isn't there. Helen waits. She goes to check if Abbi's coming. She comes back without Abbi and starts to dance alone.

H: *(moving)*

J: What're you doing?

H: *(moving)* What?

J: What're you trying to say with this?

H: *(moving)* What're you're doing?

J: Can you say that a bit louder please – *(to Goddess)* sorry can you shut up because I can't actually hear what's she saying.

Are you going to dance around again now?

H: What?

J: Are you gonna do another one of your little dances?

H: Yes… because that's the show. Shouldn't I?

J: No, because it's weird

H: Is it?

J: What's the point?

H: Why does there have to be a point?

J: Because you've asked people to come

H: Abbi

J: Who's Abbi?

H: You are

J: No I'm not

H: Are you doing your John voice? Are you being John?

J: I'm not being John, no

H: Because you are John?

   Alright, John, you shouldn't be here

J: Why?

H: Because your bit's over

J: It's unfinished

H: I know

J: Why?

H: Because life is unfinished

J: Is that the point?

H: Stop saying point

J: Stop saying nothing

H: Can we talk about this later?

J: I won't be around later

H: Why, have you got plans?

J: I'm meeting some friends for a drink after the show

H: Very funny

J: Some man friends actually, we're going to talk about man stuff

H: This is typical

J: That's kind of the point

H: Why are you doing this?

J: I've got some ideas for your show, for how you could make it better

H: Oh of course you have

J: You're clearly smart –

H: Thanks

J: I mean you can clearly use words when you want to, the bit about men at the beginning – which I don't fucking agree with – proves that

H: Uh huh

J: But then you just give up

H: It's not giving up

J: You need to be specific, if you want people to understand you

H: What am I being?

J: You need to use words if you want everyone to understand exactly what you are clearly trying to say

H: That wouldn't work

J: Why not?

H: Because the words don't exist that say exactly what I'm trying to say

.

J: That's ridiculous. There are over one million and thirty five thousand words in the the English language alone –

H: Well done, John yes there are a lot of words but they were made for you to express yourself, not me.

J: Because you're a girl?

H: Woman

J: That's bullshit, loads of girls are really good at words and out of us you should be the one to say that, not me

H: That's a different thing. Being good at it, and being facilitated by it, they are different. But this is none of your business. I don't want to make a show out of a man-made language that has hijacked my brain and stunted my imagination and do you know what? I don't have to.

J: Man made? I think a lot of the girls – sorry women – here are going to have a big fucking problem with that

H: Well they should have a big problem with that! But I'm not saying – do you know what I'm going to do it like this actually

(she takes a microphone)

I'm not saying men invented language, I'm saying they wrote it down. A man decided that Mankind would be the word for all of us. A man decided that He is more comprehensive than She. They decided that their stories were important, their metaphors were clever, their opinions, objective. That a man is a pilot and a woman is a female pilot. That there is even a right or a wrong way at all, and this is just the obvious stuff.

J: Do you want to bang your little drum again now?

H: No I'm alright thanks

J: So invent more words

H: I should. I will. But then there'll just be more words that mislead you into thinking that words can ever make you understand me. When I say love, you think we understand each other? When I say chair, do you think we're imagining the same thing – exactly the same thing? Words are blunt instruments, just like –

J: You seem fine with using words just now

H: *(blows a raspberry)*

J: I'm just trying to help

H: Stop taking space!

J: Taking?! None of this about me. It's all about you. This isn't about men. This is about what you think of men. This is not a selfless act.

H: Of course it's not. Why should it be? Everything's about you.

J: Fuck off it's about me. Or if it is, it's about how everything I am is stupid or irrelevant. You're asking me to be here so you can point and fucking laugh!

H: And this is why you're actually here. You don't give a shit about language. Look John I'm sorry your dad died and you want someone to shout at but tell me how you feel, don't tell me what to do – you're being such a man!

J: And just once I would like someone to say that and for it to be a good fucking thing! Just once, I would like Man not to mean Cunt.

H: I want to want you to be part of this but I will not let you take over.

J: Then tell me what to do

H: What?

J: ~~Dismantle me, Helen. Put me back together in the right~~ order. What should I say? What should I think? How shall I speak? How shall I move? How shall I fucking fuck? Tell me.

H: ~~It's not my job to tell you~~

J: It is your job – it is literally your job, you're at work, right now – telling me that how I am is wrong /

H: / I didn't say that

J: That I'm in crisis and I need to change. So tell me – how? Anyone can point at a mess and say MESS, but what are you going to do about it?

H: I'm not your mum, I'm not going to tell you what to do – I don't actually know – but I don't think you'd like it if I did.

J: This is a fucking waste of my time

H: No you can't go now, you've totally messed up the scene, it would be weird if you went now

.

J: Do you want me to talk about my feelings?

H: No

J: Would that help the scene?

H: Stop taking the piss

J: Shall I vomit my heart out so that you can help me come to terms with my emotions, which I could never possibly comprehend on my own?

H: We're not suggesting –

J: Who's we? I hit my dad, when I was looking after him. He was in the loo and he was throwing his shit everywhere, literally picking it up out of the toilet, and throwing it around, and I couldn't be fucked to clean up again and I was tired and I hit him. Really hard in the face, he bled. What does that say about me? What does that say about men, Helen?

H: This isn't real

J: I need you to hear me say it, so I can heal

H: I don't trust anything you say

J: I'm very attracted to you right now, I really like to fuck strong women

H: Abbi stop it I don't like it

J: What gives you the right to speak on my behalf?

H: I'm not. Abbi.

J: Hey you behind the piano, do you want to go for a drink after the show?

H: Abbi

J: Who's Abbi?

H: Abbi, I don't like it

A: Why not?

H: Because I don't understand what's happening anymore

A: I'm being a man

H: Well stop

A: I don't want to

H: Why not?

A: I think it suits me

H: Why?

A: Because I'm allowed to ahhh

H: Time to be quiet and get on with the show now

A: I have more to say

H: Later

A: I'm a man

H: You're a woman

A: I'm a man

H: You're a woman

A: I want to be a man

H: No you don't

A: No I don't but I am

H: You don't look like one

A: I know, I don't want to

H: Good

A: Balls are weird

H: Don't talk about balls

A: But on the inside

H: This is awful!

A: I like my skirt

H: You're a woman

A: I'm a man woman

H: You're a woman

A: I'm a man woman

H: What's that?

A: Me

H: Abbi!

A: Move over. Man woman looks like a woman but talks
like a man. Man woman talks direct and sometimes
takes over the room and talks like she doesn't care if
you like her or not. Man woman cares if you like her.
Man woman stuffs imaginary socks in her man woman
mouth to stop her man woman tongue from going man
woman rogue. Man woman gets described as a strong
woman. She has balls. She punches walls. She thinks
in straight lines. She thinks quick and speaks quicker.
Man woman is ambitious. Man woman likes control.
Man woman is always certain. Man woman wears
the trousers. Man woman has sex with woman man.
Woman man isn't threatened by her. He's amazing.
We all admire woman man for how he supports her.
People look at man woman out of the corner of their
eyes and say out of the corners of their mouths She's
not real. She's just pretending. She's not like that. That's
not hers. She should be soft lines and curly thoughts
and whispering about her feelings and light footsteps.
She should stand on one leg and smile. Did you notice
that? A bit of her spit just landed on my face that's
disgusting. She's getting so excited, she's spitting while
she talks. She's doesn't even stop talking to eat, she's
just talking with her mouth full of food. She's sold out.
She's pretending to be one of them. She's pretending
to be one of us. Man woman likes an argument. I'm a
man woman I'm not pretending I'm real. They didn't
invent this, this is mine and I feel. That's right I like an
argument. I like to go through the middle. I don't like
skirts and I don't like skirting round the edge. You keep
disappearing round the back and won't look me in the
eye. Where've you gone? Turn and face me. You think
I'm a bully. You think I'm a brute, I know you do.
Well I'm no brute – you're pathetic! You're being
pathetic. I can only walk all over you if you lie the fuck
down. Get up! You think gentle is kind? You think gentle
doesn't hurt? Your gentle silence slices me in the side
and then you act surprised when I bleed out. You did

that you fucking whiney fuckbag. Don't tell me to be
quiet. Don't tell me I'm showing off. Don't tell me that
I'm a control freak. I'm no freak. Don't tell me I'm
talking too loud or that I should let someone else have
a turn, I haven't finished yet. And stop telling me to stop
interrupting, I'll interrupt if I want. You should say what
you want to say quicker or louder if it's so important.
Don't expect me to sit on my tongue. I can't. I can't sit
on my tongue it's not long enough obviously! And I'm
not pretending to be like them, this is who I am. I'm not
sorry. If you want more space then you'll have to fight
for it. If you want the stage you'll have to push me out
of the way. Because I could stay here all night and it's
not because I'm pretending. I used to carry trees. Aged
five I used to carry trees. There's photographic evidence
I used to carry trees so you can't tell me I'm pretending.
You keep pointing at her and saying – gosh she's so
beautiful isn't she? She's so ladylike isn't she? She's
such a natural woman isn't she? Well I've got biceps
bigger than my breasts and I used to carry trees.
Because I don't mind a fight. Because I like to talk to
the big men like they talk to me. Because I really like
to talk to the big men like they talk to me. Because
I'm not alpha or beta, I'm fucking omega. Because
I've got stuff to fucking say. Because I'm too much?
I'm barely enough. This is me toned down. This is me
on my best behaviour. This is me being a lady. This
is as quiet as my voice goes. This is me chewing with
my mouth closed and taking care to swallow before I
speak. I could be gnawing at the bone. Fuck nodding.
Fuck being a cat. Fuck being a dog. I'm a fucking
T-Rex. I might have stupid little arms but I've got fuck-
off massive teeth and the loudest, ear-shattering,
shit-yourself-I'm-coming-and-I'm-fucking-close, roar.
Tectonic plate-shattering footsteps. Knock-the-earth-
off-its-axis-fucking-run, I'm fucking unstoppable I'm an
ogre. Fuck your dainty doilies and your piping bags and
your pore tightening ointments and your hips moving
like silk and your arpeggio of a laugh and your soft skin

and your long fingernails and your listening. Fuck your
listening! I've got too much to fucking say to fucking
listen! Your listening and your nodding and your smiling
and your understanding. NO I DON'T UNDERSTAND
YOU. I DON'T UNDERSTAND YOUR FEELINGS OR
YOUR PAIN. I DON'T WANT TO. I'm too busy thinking
and chewing and running. I'M THE FUCKING LEADER.
I'm not following you around the dance floor, you can't
even dance, you haven't even got rhythm, you don't
even know the steps. Watch me. Watch my feet. I know
this dance. I'm doing it right. I can't follow you, I don't
know where you're taking me. I don't want to know.
I don't want to close my eyes and feel with my hips and
tune in to your every move so we can move as one.
I'll take this solo. And you can run along behind.
AND I'M NOT PRETENDING. I'm real. This is real.
I'm no man. They didn't invent this. Men didn't invent
being direct or taking over a room or being a loud Cunt
who always thinks they're right. Who never listens. I did.
I invented it. It's mine. I don't got no balls. I don't got
no guts. I'm no bell curve of masculine and feminine.
I'm no yin yang. I'm no light and dark. I'm just meat
and teeth and shouting. So fuck you. Just because
I can use my body to make another human because
I'm fucking magic doesn't mean I should stroke you
when you're sad. Fuck tenderness. I like my steak
fucking tender. Send it back, it's not bloody enough.
They've ruined it! And I'll wear a dress if I want, I don't
care if I confuse you. I'll start a fight in my dress.
I'll talk with my mouth full of sequins. I'll throw you
round the dance floor in backless silk. I'll hitch it up
and tuck it in my knickers when it gets in my way and
it's mine. I'm not a strong fucking woman. I'm a fucking
woman. I don't wear the trousers, thank you. I wear
nothing. Look at my bum. Look at my muscles. Look at
my teeth. AHHHHHHHHHHHHHH.

Helen starts interrupting. They improvise an argument both grappling for the microphone.

A: Oh sorry Helen did you want the microphone?

Abbi unplugs the microphone and offers it to Helen.

H: It's alright I'll just use this one instead

She picks up a different mic.

H: I've just got a few things that I would like to say too if that's okay?

I fear I will never be a brilliant parallel parker.
I don't actually like talking about my or your bodily functions. Sorry.
My thoughts don't formulate themselves in straight and logical patterns, my opinions don't sound like facts so you won't know when to trust me.
I can't pretend I'm certain. In fact I'll never be totally certain unless I've had more alcohol than is reasonable for one human to drink.
I like it when you say that I'm a lady, I'm really good at being a lady. So good that sometimes I wish I could go back in time, and I don't want to go forwards if going forwards means I have to be like that *(she points at Abbi).*

I'd rather be

She dances like a 1950s film star.

Does anyone here think I'd be a good leader because
I don't mind doing it but not if anyone else wants to?
You should know that I don't watch the fight scenes.
I hide behind my hands and ask him to tell me when
it's over.
I still want him to be bigger and stronger than me, I still
feel safer when he's with me, sometimes I want him to
look after me.
I would say I'm made of plasticine and not concrete.
Do you know that sometimes I hold things so lightly
I drop them and it still always surprises me.
I like to let my body float rather than deciding what
to do with it.
I want to move like this

She embodies a classical femininity.

This is the place where I could have chosen to be a
T – Rex and I've decided to…meow.
No matter how much you [push] me I won't retaliate.
Yeah sorry that's probably my fault.
I'm less like a bullet train and more like a…
I'm sorry for being sorry all the time because I know I'm
not supposed to be sorry all the time I'm supposed to be
[strong unapologetic woman] and you know sometimes
I really can be *(she sings loudly into the mic)*
But I don't always want a big space and sometimes
I'm totally fine
with this *(she curls up small).*

Helen being small
(being up (John being small)

I thought I could tell you with words who I am with words
how funny of me
I thought I could tell you with words who I am with words
how funny of me
I thought I could tell you with words who I am with words
how funny of me
I thought I could tell you with words who I am with words
how funny of me

I thought I could tell you with words who I am with words
how funny of me
I thought I could tell you with words who I am with words
how funny of me
I thought I could tell you with words who I am with words
how funny of me
I thought I could tell you with words who I am with words
how funny of me

I wake you up in the middle of the night to ask what
it's like to be you
I wake you up in the middle of the night to ask what
it's like to be you
I wake you up in the middle of the night to tell you
I'm not scared of who you really are
I wake you up in the middle of the night to tell you
I'm not scared of who you really are

I thought I could tell you with words who I am with words
how funny of me
I thought I could tell you with words who I am with words
how funny of me

I wake you up in the middle of the night to ask what
it's like to be you
I wake you up in the middle of the night to tell you
I'm not scared of who you really are
I thought I could tell you with words who I am with words
how funny of me

I thought I could tell you with words who I am with words
how funny of me
I thought I could tell you with words who I am with words
how funny of me

End.

WWW.OBERONBOOKS.COM

Printed in the USA
CPSIA information can be obtained
at www.ICGtesting.com
LVHW020934171024
794056LV00003B/756